T0102697

THINGS CIRCULAR

Cissus World Press Poetry Series

THINGS CIRCULAR

Poems in this collection use themes of love, nostalgia, nature and experiences to create a timeless cultural guide and lesson on life.

Lupenga Mphande

THINGS CIRCULAR. Copyright © Lupenga Mphande, 2015.

All rights reserved.
Manufactured in the United States of America.

Except in the case of brief quotations included in critical articles or reviews, no portions of this book may be reproduced without written permission.

Publisher's information, address:
Cissus World Press, P.O.Box 240865, Milwaukee, WI 53224
www.cissusworldpressbooks.com

First published in the U.S.A by Cissus World Press
ISBN: 978-0-9679511-7-1

Cover Design: Dike Okoro
Cover photo: Lupenga Mphande

CISSUS WORLD PRESS books are published by Dike Okoro, Founding Publisher.

Abstract

Lupenga Mphande delineates how poetry offers vital and meaningful theoretical models for conceptualizing our relationship as human beings to the natural world, and his poems explore the spaces of a shared experience of memory and family and nature.

Dedication

In memory of my father and mother,
to *Hlupekile* and your silent inspiration,
to *Leya*, *Tamaliyapo*, and *Tawonga*
for your love and support
and to all the youths of Thoza
I dedicate these poems to you.

Acknowledgments

Poetry Review (UK) – "The victim"

Songs for Wonodi – "Rain dance;" "Vuso"

Poems Deep and Dangerous – "Why the old woman limps"

The haunting wind: – "Through the thicket," "Canopied foliage."

When my brothers come home – "Song of a prison guard," "When the storms come."

Bending the bow – "I want to be all things to you," "Waiting for you."

Table of contents

Walking the plateau

I can't look at all at these lush fields of Hoho
Without thinking of Kaliyangile, the hermit
Who cultivated millet, pumpkin, and musaka
To chase away kwashiorkor from his village,
I can't look over the rolling plateaus beyond,
The tree-clad banks and green reeds
Without thinking of Chimbekeya, the blacksmith
Who molded guns, made gunpowder from goat dung
And, in season, taught me how to hunt with the bee,
Feed with the otter ... I cannot at all walk through
The Vipya and watch hippopotami in placid lagoons,
Slithering, appearing and disappearing in gambols,
Or river fish shooting out of water and shooting back again,
Or cranes, flamingoes, pelicans, herons, kingfishers scudding
Along river banks, and flocks of small birds, brilliant and swift
Flash from reeds, rise out of sight - I can't watch all this
Without thinking of the Dwambazi of my childhood.

A stroll to the hills

Frustrated in my numerous attempts at poetry writing,
Determined to seek solace and quietude in the tranquil countryside,
And cognizant of my visitor's desire for morning fresh air and fun
I abandoned my writing pen, and picked up my walking stick.
What else could one do in the quiet of the morning but turn for hills
That line the valley behind our village, shaded by sunlit
Ridges and filled with birdsong and yodeling of herd's boys,
Painting a vague sensation of awaiting pleasures.
Remnants, perhaps, of an ancient glacier that grazed the earth
The valley is strewn with tawny scraps of rocks and craggy hillocks.
It is there that I took my visitor for a stroll,
Walking through thickets and stunted bushes up a bluff
To a rock cave where the ancients left their mark long ago,
Now sheltering snakes, leopards, hyenas and city bandits. It wasn't
That I ignored the kids' warning that leopards and pythons
That feed on rock rabbits live there, but these are old stories
Parents tell their children to keep them at home
For changes in weather patterns have scuttled all those creatures
To better places, or extinction. In any case,
Boredom in Thoza seals your fate to take the risk.

As the hot sun shone down on the valley
We descended the ridge, passed the reed beds, and crossed the river.
We went upstream for a while, then veered east and ascended a hillock,
Scaling the scraggy surface through mountain rabbit paths,
Zigzagging up rock boulders to the summit,
Past a stagger of *miombo* trees hanging over the ancient cave
Where gregarious weaverbirds gather twigs for their nests.
I craned my neck to look up the big *muyombo* tree, its leaves silhouetted
Against the sky, their color merging with the blue, its ancient trunk
Charred by forest fires and scarred over by cavities left by bee hunters,
And its ranching roots fused into the seams of the rocks.
I craned further forward to get a better view of a bird's nest on a branch,
But it was too far and I abandoned the attempt.
I glanced at the brook across that feeds into the valley
And stared for a long time at the hillocks that sparkled against the sun.
Their rocks looked so familiar, sparkling against the foliage.

I thought of a time long ago when earth was being shaped
And the sluggish glacier scooped out the soil around these rocks
Leaving them jutting stumps over the valley, forlorn, bereft of soil.
I wasn't sure how long the muyombo has been left standing like this,
Lonely, its roots forced to fuse with the surrounding granite.
A baby cried in the distance, no doubt awakened by the gregarious calls
Of the weaverbirds and the wisp of breeze whistling through the hill pass.
The baby's mother, who cannot fuse with the soil she stands on,
Must till the sediment left by the glacier and plant seeds to feed her baby.
"Can't we watch the sunset for an extended length of time from here?"
My visitor inquired in the waning sunlight, her voice rising against the breeze.
I looked at the shadows around us, and looked at her.
"The mountain rabbits and their predators are about to come out," I said.
And I saw how dark it will soon be, and late.

Hill people

As the clouds parted, sunlight
Scraped the hills, hardened,
And turned into haze.
Years from now, when all is told
Our children will say
We lived a full life among these hills

Living in unison with nature's dictates
Listening to the twitter of birds as they scuttle
To feed in the fields of the valley lash with grain
Our children will rejoice, glad to have sat
Under the shadows of the hills

Buds of new fronds will glow gold
In the sunlight, and the bees and wind
Will carry afar songs of our freedom
And when all is told, their hummed buzz
Will gladden our hearts as hill people

But beyond the lash and green
Where the sun sets, I hear
There are no bird songs there
Just charred stumps of dead trees
The land having hardened and turned gray

Looking back – something happened there

This land, the land of plateaus, lakes, and rivers
Where the moon runs crescent into red clouds
Where neighbors seek succor in time of strife
Where rain drizzles smooth over human bickering,
This land is my land, our land, left to us
By the toil of our ancestors, the sweat of our people.

This land, the land of shimmering restless green
Where towering ranges of hills trail to the lake
This land of undulating ridges where I was born
Where villagers tend to their crops, the children their chores,
Where elders listen to birdsongs for signs of the solstice, this land
Where everything is to be remembered.

This land, our land, where tyranny once struck, like lightning,
Where people cowered down, their hopes covered in tears,
Where shimmers of the lake dimmed, like something unknown,
Like rain that catches you on a field with no shelter,
Where leaders dreaded daylight, became devious and corrupt,
Where men derided their wives, children their parents …

This land where, to this day, the police spread hate, prize firing
On unarmed protesters, where exiles bring messages of factious despair,
Our land, this land, covered in the red of martyrs …
If we had known then what we know now, shouldn't we
Have acted quickly enough to stop oppression? But no wisdom
Would have altered our fate, for emaciation is not an act of bravery.

Nthumbuzga

To be sure, we, the village kids, loved the *nthumbuzga* fruit
The season's delight, the delicacy of Thoza.
As the countryside filled with bloom and colors
We scattered at the edge of the woods, like hares,
Scouring for the juicy pink flesh-colored fruit
Amidst the twitter of birds, their beaks stained red.

About the *nthumbuzga* fruit, what shall I say?
It makes me sad, Tamaliyapo, my daughter,
That you haven't tasted the delicious juicy pulp of the season
For you have never lived in a village at the edge of the woods.
When picked ripe and served at dinner table, red trickling
From its flesh – the thought of it evokes a burning thirst!

Today you can buy many fruits in supermarkets, my daughter,
But avoid bitter ones that upset the stomach:
Fruit picked from trees blighted by drought,
Fruit plucked unripe at tropical harvest season
Fruit kept green in preservatives of sugar glaze
And sour fruit from whose juice milk curd is made.

I prefer the *nthumbuzga* fruit because its taste is succulent
And hidden, its rind the color of the rainbow,
Its blossom deeply enfolded, its fragrance pleasant,
And its flowers in bloom delightful. I'll compose a song
Dedicated to the *nthumbuzga* fruit, my daughter,
And sung whenever the woods turn into season.

uZolozolo: my favorite bird

I see you in the morning rays, *uzolozolo*, on the lawn
Behind my house, hopping about among the flower beds
Probing in soft earth, continuously rooting out grubs from
Leaf litter. Welcome to my yard, *uzolozolo*, migratory bird,
Let me steer you away from garden weeds and pesticides
And guide you to the bushy grove across the creek.

Glossy bird: brick-orange your mantle, your wing shoulders
Broad, striking black-and-white, your bill long and down-curved,
Your crest and wing feathers, which explode into a riot of colors
When you are excited, pinkish-brown, strongly barred with
White cream. A white bar runs across your tail base and, in flight,
Like a butterfly, your rounded pied wings buff up your size.

If you're hungry and raise your low-pitched *hoop ... hoop* call
I'll lead you to the open acacia woodland beyond the creek
Abundant in beetles, caterpillars, and larvae, and together
We'll fly from tree to tree, searching bark and limbs for insects,
We'll refurbish unsealed willow tree cavities for nesting.

And if it interests you we will move to the gallery forest
And ascend to the treetop. Should intruders approach,
We will fold into a broad front and break out in a cackle,
Dressed head-to-toe in buff-orange gear with black-tipped
Feathers, and, like doves in season, like butterflies in spring,
Holding onto each other, we'll soar high above the woods
And frolic about the woodlands, in the morning air,
I safely tucked under your wings, forever yours.

- *uzolozolo* (in Zulu) hoopoe, a colorful tropical bird

Moving on

I watched the afternoon sun's rays
fall silently on dry leaves
as termites mauled around them.
Here and there, something else
stirred the leaves
and I knew it was time to go.

Tree shadows lolled from where they had fallen.
Easterly, towards the Thoza hills on the horizon
I saw the footmarks of a lone duiker leading
to the waterhole beyond the anthill.
It's so late in life to have so few friends.

A weak breeze whiffed past
as I ascended the *musuku* slope
back to the village, and I heard *mpapa* ponds
split, broadcasting their seeds to eternity.
It's time for regeneration, time for renewal.

The moon rose over the hills in a cloudless sky
and the evening drifted on the wind.
All over the ridge fires flared into festive bursts,
making the stars in the sky look uneventful. I knew
it was time to bid farewell, time for the next in line.

Rain dance

It was a horrible drought dusk
that littered the hot land with wilted plants
and desiccated carcasses of game.
God in His remote universe,
commanded by no one,
who knows our needs and desires
but chooses His own accord to act,
(or not act), nonetheless sent children
to pray to Him for rain -
it made no difference
except to fulminate against His idleness.

Next morning
we turned our eyes to the eland bull,
combatants with bow and arrows
slung across our shoulders.
We stalked the eland in the thickets
thrashed the eland from cobwebbed anthills
chased the eland across the veldt,
and cornered the eland in the river bend.
Some stood and clapped as we encircled him,
and others, with gushing nose-bleeds, slumped
to the floor of the riverbed on their backs.
We held the eland at bay.

Defiant, the great beast plunged.
We gasped! Echoes ringing in our ears
we stood there, speechless.
Our elders pondered: the bull has to be pulled
from the depths - brought ashore to soak the earth.
Amidst shrieks of hornbills, ululations of women,
and exaltations of something beautiful captured
we pulled him from the water, dripping,
led him over dry and dusty fields,

his horns spiraling heavenwards,
like a pair of honeyed owls pecking at the sky.
"Wherever the eland will tread," we had learned,
"clouds will form and rain fall for the bull
As never fallen before.
Wild onions will sprout around river pools,
bees come to taste dew drops between sepals
antelopes stampede at waterholes
and soon the countryside will be lush
with green fields, laughter,
and songs of birds in tree groves."

Hastening to the pool in the hot sun
sheen of their seashell necklaces glimmering
in flashes of lightning like fireflies,
a retinue of village initiates presented their faces
painted in the thunder red of ochre,
their conical nipples hardening against the haze,
their waist beads jiggling in unison
with vibrating riverbed reeds.

They were indifferent at the sacrifice,
concelebrants at the poolside.
Initiates paused before leaping
over the still body of the eland, the rain giver,
and stared into its tearful glassy eyes.
They saw their own faces.
God, they remembered,
is commanded by no one
brooks no rival.
The bull, they knew, had to die.

A land locked people

The wind lashes through the *mupapa* trees
The leaves whistling as they sway to the mountain
Wind, hushing the chitterling of the woodpeckers
That hitch up tree trunks, incessantly chiseling for grubs.
When the lake lashes with assiduous force on a treeless shore
Whizzing of the wind is muted, its rhythm almost meaningless.
On the plateau, many miles from the shore, standing trees
Break the urgency of the wind, the lash through trees
Reverberates over the plateau, re-echoing back the roaring lake
Through brooks that connect a land locked people to the shore.
Clouds gather and throw shadows over mountain foliage.
I listen to the wind, but will tell no one
About my bad dream in which the waves lashed the shore
And capsized the fishermen's canoes on the lake
Sowing disaster in its wake, toppling dwellings,
Careening water vessels, upturning fish racks. ...

For we are a land locked people at the mercy of a haughty lake
A lake with angry waves that lash the shore and spew foam,
A lake with waves that lash with assiduous force, capsizing canoes
A lake whose shimmers flame in the rising sun and swirl of lagoons
A lake with currents measured in tides of the moon ...
For we are a breed that weaves palm fronds into baskets
A breed, perched between the hills and the twitter of birds
A breed that harnesses a downpour for our rice fields along the shore
A breed that stakes its claim to the lake with its oars – for we are
Endowed with varieties of fresh water fishes – and
Chronicle our people's memories into stories for our children.
We are a people from the warm heart of Africa
That buries the past in our sleep and leaves songs of our valor
To our children, for the world is frail
And needs the potent of our tongue.

A road through the plateau

They opened a road through the plateau, a broad striped road,
A bituminized road spawning steel bridges and cement culverts –
Locals called it *mtola mahule*; Cecil Rhodes, to subdue the natives
In the name of the empire, branded it the red insignia:
The *Great North Road*, proclaiming, *Lux in tenebris,*
They blasted rocks in the fragrant countryside with Nobel's
Dynamites and cut the wood covering the hills with saw chains
And earthmovers to open up the swath through the plateau

Like a famished snake in a cave with no mice to feed on
The road meanders through the plateau to a non-destination
Criss-crossing the landscape and crosscutting mountains
Sluicing the countryside with gravel pits and carcasses of game
And scattering, like fragments of dust, dried bones of those
That stood in its way, for they have dug up the hills
To get niobium and rare earth deposits underneath the rocks
Exposing villagers to foreign ways and an eerie tranquilized calm

Where before the white sky was blue at its edges,
The horizon green beyond the trail of hills toward the lake,
Now the edge of the sky has hazed over with dynamite fumes.
And somewhere inside a tree line of euphorbia and acacia
Where the eland galloped, nibbled *miombo* foliage,
And birds whistled around their nests, now articulated trucks
Screech along, loaded with corporations' supplies.
Fleets of antelopes with their fledglings that rained the plateau
Have fled corporate game hunters and their marksman rifles

I drove through the plateau one night around midnight,
As the lake breeze whizzed by, cooling the asphalt
On the road; I saw in the night air from time to time
Flashes of fireflies, red eyes of nightjars and spotted owls,
Harbingers of dawn, hooting their mournful song; I saw also
Wailing lesser bush babies huddled together, and I couldn't tell
If they were laughing or crying – and if you must know,
They were gravely grieved over the foggy expanse of the road.
I wouldn't have believed it possible if I hadn't seen it happen.

Tingle of memories

There is a lone house
On the cone of an anthill
In a remote part of Perekezi forest,
The path that winds up to it
Looks rarely used.

I lost my way there once
Seeking shelter from a tropical hailstorm,
A herd's boy caught in unpredicted weather
Stranded in Perekezi forest.

What a day it was!
I said to no one.
What a day it was indeed
I say it again today.

The woods go on forever
And at the thought of it still I feel a tingle
Around the corner of my mouth
Twitching the lips into a smile.

Matanje – the plateau people

They lived on the plateau, the *Matanje* people,
And claimed they came out of the earth and lived off the land.
They roamed the plateau, hunted game, flayed carcasses for cloth,
Weaved palm fronds into baskets, and tamed wild dogs for sport.

They thought a man rich with two hoes, bark cloth, a basket
Full of seashells, and a gourd of sesame oil to rub on their wounds –
For the land was lush, game plentiful, famine rare, and people
Minded their chores, mended thatch and tilled the soil.

The countryside was glazed with sunlight, and there was mist and haze.
During times of thunderclaps, every bird headed to its nest, women sowed
Their seeds in the sediment, cultivated their fields dotting the valley,
Made them meek, their work songs rending the noon air.

They celebrated their achievements in song and dance, mindful of vainglory
That breeds resentment – for they were *Matanje*, who came out of the earth,
And lived off the land. They trapped winged termites, conscious the enemy
Was not just the bore-weevil that fed on grain and destroyed their crops.

Seeking a bond to the past, they tussled with nature over resources,
Built a tower on the mist-covered *Jenjewe* Mountain to reach the sky
And escape the flood on land. But when their heads touched the clouds
The tower collapsed – the termites had eaten away the base.

At the fireside, elders told fabulous tales that enthralled the children,
Filling the evening with laughter – for they were a fair people, grateful to
Their ancestors buried in the past of the earth. They knew well enough
Not to rush into the future leaving their hearths unattended, for the enemy
Were the termites that had eaten away the core of their base. They knew also
That, when yellow leaves fall, gold buds couldn't be far behind.

Standing still, side by side

It was in May, at ripening grass that the child was born
When birds and wild hogs invade millet and corn fields
To joyride and feast on the grain.
To guard their crops, the man built a mock shelter around
His field, and his wife and he stood guard by night and day,
Serene and in control, like wild plateau grasses, unwavering,
Shielding their infant against pestering drizzles and howling
Mountain winds. They stood there besides each other
In a mock hermit by the hillside in the field of corn,
Warriors battling the elements! That is when the child was born,
In May, and they named him, 'the last post,' *lupenga*.

The whole force of easterly winds and misty drizzles
Charged against them. But they, together, hand in hand,
Faced the elements, silhouetted against a moonlit
Darkness and a billowing breeze, and glazed against the hill
Where the corn-ravaging wild pigs seemed to originate.
Determined to stand their ground and protect what was theirs,
The infant tightly cradled to their bosoms, they hoped
One day, as firstborn, in accordance with belief, the infant
Would grow to be a man and fend off rainstorms and hogs,
And thus help farmers tend to their fields in peace.

And so it was that they stood there, side by side,
The infant cradled in their hold.
What they said to each other I do not know,
What they thought about the infant I can only imagine,
And I stand here to pay silent homage to the bravery of
Two lovers by a grass thatched shelter, holding hands,
Their infant snuggled against the chill of easterly mountain winds.
For they were two lovers with great expectation for their child -
My father and mother too: two devoted parents rest peacefully
Lying side by side in a shed of *miombo* trees by the creek
Silent under the easterly wind that sways the leaves.

Writing to my mother

Anxious and eager to boast to my mother
About what we have learned at school today,
But with neither pen nor paper to write on,
I stop by a patch of fine sand in the schoolyard
Flatten the sand with my palm,
And set down to write her a letter with my fingertip.
I tell her what our teacher told us in class
About the first woman on earth
And the footmarks she left behind,
About the man on the moon
And the rocks he brought back,
About addition, and subtraction,
About division and multiplication,
About how water is formed
And the explosion that can annihilate mankind ...
What a maze the figures make on sand!
To conclude the letter,
I ask my mother for forgiveness
For the things I left undone:
The thatch she wanted mended
The yard she wanted swept
The cow she wanted milked
The children she wanted washed and fed
The garden weeded, the bean vegetables plucked ...
And the many other chores around the home
I didn't do because I'd have been late for school.
But alas! With no paper, stamp nor envelope,
And the post office being far away,
Will the wind deliver the letter to my mother?
Or will it for ever remain
Shredded into these tiny particles of sand?

Thoza made me

I wandered barefoot, tending to herds in creeks
Where swallows abound. How fortunate!
A youth for whom the earth held great promise
Born when the big war was over
With millions dead, many more wounded
Surrounded by well wishers
In a season of festive welcome. How fortunate!

Cattle range the hillside, devouring tendrils of shrubs,
Flocks of birds flush from patches of ripening grass,
And sets of herd's boys yodel in the woods. Awesome!
But soon calls of orioles in the woodland are superseded
By groans of people afflicted with the dreaded disease,
A village emptied by a silence no birdcall can break.

Thoza made me, and no lesser a place. The memory
Of those that went before us stir a valiant pride in my heart.
When all is told and done, and our life advances towards its end,
Please lay me down in the village yard below the anthill.
I will take my sleep in those sandy soils where my life began
Where my father and mother and young brother await for me.

The wood-cutter

When I arrived some clansmen had already come,
Their misty coughs sand muffled whispers permeating
Through the quiet of the valley, punctuating songs of bulbuls.
This is the season of shift cultivation, said one,
These deciduous trees have to be cut and set alight
Before they shed, and let the humus nurture the millet.
I shivered, waiting for the sun to light up the task;

Nothing could have pleased Yada more: his axe unslung
He leapt up the large tree that flanked the anthill
Looping from branch to branch sizing up the boughs,
His axe flashing in the sun's rays as it swung,
And ate into ebony rind, the breeze whizzing,
Throwing Yada's clothes in waves of wrestling
Cruciform shadows on the foliage;

Glistening in morning sun, he whistled out sweat
Streaming down his face, breathing in quick thuds
As he chopped branches one by one, until the last
Crashed into the undergrowth releasing a great wind.
Cloyed by the waft of crushed aloes flowering late,
I wondered which side a severed tree trunk falls
And imagined a weatherman trapped by a storm un-forecast.

Think of me

When you go to Thoza
look at the conical hills
that straddle the place where I was born
and think of me, dear friend.
Think of the stillness of a frosty winter dawn
the rustle of reeds in the tide
the lustrous colors of leaves fallen
the change of seasons and start of bushfires
the flash of starling among figs
the cooing of doves, and chirp of grasshoppers
and think of me, the herds boy
who grazed his herd by the bluff near
the lightening-stricken *muwula* tree
and loitered too long gazing at the crescent moon
until they had to go and find him. Think of me
and do not let me die

Escape from the rhinoceros

I was the herd boy that looked after the goats along the Dwambazi
While my grandmother, at eighty, after her husband had died of leukemia
Picked musaka leaves from anthills staggered throughout her garden.
She told us a funny story of having to run from a grunting rhinoceros
That invaded her village while my mother was ill with malaria.
The rhinoceros roared and grunted, she said, while she and others ducked
Through the thickets, with me strapped on her back. I have always wondered
How an old woman such as my grandmother, with me strapped on her back,
Would so easily have evaded a grunting rhinoceros in the bush. Grandma knew
That if my mother died, her only child, she would be back childless,
And would be strapped on her back the infant and the goats in the enclosure,
And the black rhinoceros still puffing and grunting in the woods. But you know,
While puffing and grunting, someone put him down with an arrow,
And my mother survived the malaria, and the woods released the spores
That fell on the ground silently, and I grew to look after the village.
When I was in college long after my grandmother had passed, I dreamt
Of the rhinoceros, puffing and grunting, charging through the thickets,
And I, a village marksman, darting from thicket to thicket with my bow.

My father and I

Up the craggy hills, through desolate streams
After years abroad, I decided to go for a walk
Through the white haze with my father
And see again the places I grew to be a man.

We veered up Thoza hill, now bereft of its lush by fire setters,
Trash-and-burn cultivators, and charcoal vendors;
Across the creek we came to where there was once a water hole,
Now dry, with streaks of sand and charred tree stumps.

We walked up the bend of the stream to an old tree with a cavity
And heard bees hum in the *kankhande* tree in flower.
I remembered how my father and I, scouring about these woods
For honey, came to this same tree one noonday, long ago.

We'd looked for bee colonies in every thicket of the hills, my father and I
Until a swooping bee-eater brought us to this scrubby bend of the stream,
We set the fire to smoke the bees out, that long ago. And, like a honey-badger,
My father took the honeycombs out one by one. And then he fell silent.

I couldn't help think that there was something he wanted to say to me.
When I flinched from a sting on my arm, my father said, half laughing,
"That's the way you learn a honey badger's skills, sonny. That's the way."
After years in exile, there was something about him I couldn't fathom,
Something to do with grace that distinguishes strength from power …

We packed the combs in leaf wrappers and we headed home. It was sad,
I thought, to leave the tree cavity empty, its trunk charred. But I was glad
That, after years of exile, I could still hear my father's tender voice, whatever
Was on his mind, glad to have treaded the hills with him, a signet of his race.

My uncle's anvil

My uncle had left the village at a young age as a carrier corps in the war
From which he learned blacksmithing as his chosen craft
– More elegantly trinket making -
His wares, when business was brisk, a favorite site at the anvil-and-harvest shows
Where bayonets, reaping knives, and spears were his signet displays.

Times being hard, trinket sales meager, and no cattle to pay lobola
My uncle had to walk thousands of miles to Cape Town on foot
– More often at night –
To find work and money to buy cattle to pay for a bride
And work was hard, pay little, and my uncle did not return.

Before he left my uncle, in his idle time, buried the anvil, hammers,
And bellow pipe behind the shed, promising to resume his trade upon his return
– More aptly when lobola was paid, the bride delivered –
But the ennui of Cape Town ushered him to city life and he died of it.
All around villagers urged me to revive my uncle's craft.

My uncle's body was not brought home to be interred where his ancestors lie
At the mourning for his death his spear was place on my shoulders:
– More accurately a successor to his homestead –
Having no children of his own, I was his next of kin, in line to inherit his craft.
I set out to retrieve the tools of his trade: anvil, hammers, bellows and all.

During my studies abroad the bellow rotted away, hummers rusted, as did the pipes
And I returned to a village in a frightful scene of dislocation
–   There still being no cattle to pay for a bride –

A year on, the new bellows murmured in remembrance of my uncle
For I was first in line and my uncle had no children of his own.

The neighbors

My father, a neighborly person, surveyed his corn plot.
"Our new neighbors have encroached on our land," he said.
"And our yield will be poor. I'll walk across the creek
To straighten things up, and it may be sometime."
He handed me his hoe and hurried across the creek to engage
Those close neighbors of ours, and left me take his place.

Weeds are persistent. The trick is to expose their roots
And take away the soil before they spread. I uprooted the weeds
Applied fertilizer, mended contour ridges in the bean garden
The way my father had instructed, and prepared the rest of the land
To lie fallow for next season ... The work was hard and the next yield
Promising, but it grew late, and my father still would not return.

Sphere of the sacred

The solitary *muwula* tree sways in the wind at full moon,
A sphere of the sacred, its branches cracking, its fruits falling
To the ground, startling from their roost nightjars
Camouflaged on fallen leaves at the edge of a leaf-litter.
Wailing with grief, children lament for your return, in another form,
Reminding us of your departure and transition to another sphere.

At dawn you set us on this long life-journey, cheered on
By your tales of wisdom and valor of those gone before us
And with prideful delight we stand now in awe of our glorious past.
You taught us that the way forward is not to look backward
Lest darkness of the past descends on our future and seed clouds
Of dark rain and factious despair and mar our new beginning.

From embers of a hearth unquenched, sparks erupt into rapturous
Articles of our birthright; we must push the rolling shatters
Of darkness to hasten dawn, lift our people from their slumber.
We must restore our people's aspirations; spur them on to greater
Heights of existence – we must not betray the trust of our ancestors,
But instill in our offspring the faith in our way of life, our heritage.

Erecting a stone to my father

A somber shadow, thicker than rain clouds in December
Fell over Thoza at my father's passing, spreading over the base
Of the hill like a bird that has flown too close to the sun.
Although it was noon, mothers tucked their children in bed,
Afraid of the descending darkness, and solemnly grieved
At my father's passing, women in white-and-black
Village choir attire shuffled their feet into a chanted dirge,
Rolling to the right, and rolling to the left in hummed tunes,
Ululating, jubilating, celebrating a life well lived –
For my father was the sage of the village, beloved by all.
Afterwards we trudged through grass to the village yard,
And when our respects were paid we filed back home
To a wakeful night spent in meditation for a life well lived.

As luminous dawn tightened into a cold spell over the ridges
Wema, my dear friend said the night before my father died
She had stayed up late talking to him by his bedside.
"He talked so much of you," she said.
A hawk soared above the hill, riding the winds,
A wagtail, my father's totem, fluttered in its communal roost
Dovetailed on rooftop like a sentry – an omen, perhaps,
Of turbulence ahead for a village forlorn, left leaderless.
At the edge of the village, trees too had shed their green coats,
As if to signal the summer of things ending;
Graying leaves had fallen to coalesce around the anthill side
Where my father held parley with disputing villagers – for he was
The best I have seen, he loved all that was to be loved.

In the village square, by the anthill, in the shade of *miombo* trees
Where morning dew lingers, where the cool gathers during the day,
I thought of erecting a stone there, where he lies,
And curve on it his name in remembrance to his life.
The village adored him, children shambled up to his embrace
Whenever they gathered to listen to his stories of old –

For he was the sage of the ridges, the beloved of the youth ...
But soon, soaked in dew, the stone will erode and chip away,
The curved name of the dead will fade and sink into oblivion,
While my father's life was incorruptible, an unfading rapture of love.
I'll mold my father's life story into a song,
Sung whenever the village children turn to this page.

The story of my father

I often narrate the story of my father to my daughter,
Reading by her bedside. I tell her that her grandfather
Always measured his words with his stick, gingerly,
That sometimes he'd tap the ground with his foot
Before the words came out in his soft voice.
"The way forward," he would say, "is to stick together."
And all at the arena would nod, as surely was his stick,
Convinced of the wisdom of his words. My father, I would say,
Loved entertaining the village children with old stories
And the children loved him back and mobbed him
Wherever he went. On other days, I would add, my father
Would pick up his axe and head to the fields to clear
The woods, or, if dressed in his Sunday wear (a suit and hat),
He would pick up his stick for downtown Thoza.
I see him now, I say to her, in his grandchildren,
And ponder again and again, with a boy's wonder,
Which way he went out in that soft voice:
Axe on his shoulder, or stick in his hand,
Tapping on the hard earth he strode on.

He left when I was away, I tell my daughter,
Studying abroad.
I hear they buried him with his stick
But put the axe on top of the grave
As if they thought he wouldn't need it.
My father was popular among his peers too,
Judging from their epitaph at his funeral.
I pause, and then turn to stories in the book,
Holding the text against the candle light,
Listening to the rustle of the wind outside.
"Dad," my daughter says,
"So which way did grandpa go?"
I don't know what to say to her.
"I was away at the time," I say.

I fumble around a little, close the book,
And blow out the candle.
I pause by the awning outside the door and stare
Into the luminous crescent night, thinking
I hear a tap, faint, on the hard earth.

Straying off too far (for my mother)

Following my fatigued shadow, returning from midnight revels,
I walked through the woods late in the moonlight
And stopped at the fork of the footpath, uncertain about the way home.
In the descending hush and flashing of fireflies
I felt a tap on my shoulder, a furtive gentle tag. I started up,
And in a moment of time, I turned and looked back.
No one was there.

A weak breeze whooshed in the *muyombo* tree above
Swaying its branches and shaking off its leaves,
Its boughs silhouetted against the moon
Its leaves' celestial shadows dancing on the grass
Between bars of fragile light shades ...
Then I glanced over my shoulder – and there,
A large yellowish leaf, withered at the edges,
Had glided onto the label of my coat!
Soon it was blown back into the breeze, and, like a lunar moth,
It whirled against the incessant whistling of the wind,
Spreading its luminous glow in the moon light.

More leaves from the surrounding *miombo* trees
Also floated around in the night air, like fireflies,
And disappeared towards the way I needed to be going.
I remembered my late mother, whenever I was late,
Glowering under her grass thatched verandah
Railing away: "Don't stray off too far into the dark!"
I hurried home, spurred on by those flares in the night.

****

30

Song of a prison guard

I see you, prisoner of Dzeleka,
From behind this hole here in the door panel;
I lurk along the hum of cicadas and mosquitoes
In moon shades of corn stalks and banana leaves
And shadows of barbed-wire posts and farm ridges –
I hide behind this iron cleft, and peep
Into your cell like a Cyclops, unseen –
I am guard to this valley prison camp.

Your little room, prisoner of Dzeleka,
Will grow forever small, your life in the lurch to waste
And cluck at the wind; even at night I will keep you awake
With the dry double lock designed to lacerate your sleep.
Don't tell me the political layout of your crimes,
I only stoke up furnaces for those I receive to roast
In chilly cells, and whet the axe for the condemned
To throttle at the gallows like a chick with its head off –
I am the guard charged with executions.

Do you see that window up the cell wall, prisoner
Of Dzeleka? Of course it's too small and will forever
Grow smaller, but look out sometimes on fine days.
If you find it painful to see children at play, and
Watch the life you've so unwittingly deserted, study:
Count threads in a cobweb; rate the beams in a ray from
The crack on the eastern wall at daybreak,
Study the ray that lingers on after nightfall,
Study the strands in a life that's lost its shadow, study …

And when you discover the beam-wave that relates to your pain
Hum in harmony with cicadas and mosquitoes in the shade,
Celebrate the merger of darkness with midnight, do a dirge
To gods of swaps and hill caves, take three steps forward

Then backward and swerve – left right right left –
Weather changes in circles, dawn ousts darkness … Tropical
Summers are hot, but your cell will be a cold, cold winter:
You'll live in that narrow room to the final night.
It's like a piece of thread on which our days hang,
To fall away, one after another, wasted.

Through the thicket

Herds of cattle and goats move slowly across the hillside
And pause to look like red and white blossom on a village tree,
A cloud of shadows brings life to the far off hills as I watch.
There is silence in the valley, yet not complete silence
For the Maharawunda valley is never quiet all winter
As oxen moo and ploughs tear through loam earth.
Another shadow crosses the valley, whirls away, returns, pauses,
Curiously seeking, hovers for a long time, then makes a sudden
Sweep to take away a safely dead mouse – down here nothing is wasted.
In the katope trees above a dove purrs from unshed leaves,
Rockets into the sky, pauses at the apex, and tumbles back
Into song: love is coming, courting time is almost here …
His urge is like that of a man when his blood is young and stirred.
In youth the future is like a hazy hill in the dawn light of winter
When fog in riverside deciduous trees propitiated glory in a winter day.

Living under sealed borders

We live under sealed borders
Gunfire marking out our perimeters

Agents of the regime billet on exile residents
Or go in disguise to their social functions –
The entire Mkwapatila Mhango family perished

Knowing we all like to be forgiven
For our acquiescence in the sins of one man
Silencing the rest.

Martyr's day

On martyr's day pupils sing of heroes whose blood
Was shed for our freedom: John Chilembwe
Was beheaded by British soldiers
For defending his people against colonial bondage,
At Nkhata Bay men and women were mowed down
On quay for daring to sing freedom songs,
Yatuta Chisiza, with his comrades, to the last man standing,
Stood their ground gallantly against all odds at Neno
In defense of what they held sacred – "I am a soldier,"
Chisiza declared, "and I do not stab from the back."
Pardon my omissions, for there are many more
Unsung heroes that died in Banda's jails
For daring to oppose tyranny, challenging those
Who stood to benefit from oppression.
Detained students, writers, and artists come to mind:
They rose in their droves against commanders of terror
And paid the price. I condemn as despicable
Those who sit on the fence when human rights are violated,
Those who are paid to defend the wicked acts of those in power
Those who bury their heads in the sand – I mean the hangers-on,
Tavern lovers that deaden their conscience, the walking dead of
Our time who acquiescence in sins of oppression.
I will not sing a single praise song for them.

They say we are traitors

They say we are traitors, those of us
Who record what we see.
Many have been jailed, condemned to prison farms,
Or caged in chains and shackled
To shiver and cluck like chicken
And the rest have been shot,
Their bodies left in rivers for crocodiles.

How long will a people
Be denied freedom and the pursuit of happiness?
Not for long!
People will rise up the country over
And free air will once more blow easy in the villages.

Mzuzu police

It is July, the beginning of winter in Mzuzu,
The plateau city of serene green
Where the bustle of Tonga fish vendors
Merge with smell of Indian garlic, saturated
Samsa, and the sound of the muezzin...
Swahili merchants in their bright *khanga* cloths talk
Uninterruptedly to their customers about bribery
And police brutality at the expense of truth –
They hate the Mzuzu police, they say.

It does not help that recently college students
And unemployed youths protesting against
Government policies and economic hardships
Were mowed down into pools of blood across the streets
By Mzuzu police officers, gone berserk with their rifles.
The president and some parliamentarians talked
With glee on national television and radio stations,
Blaming the young men and women for their own deaths –
Provocateurs, they said, have to be smoked out!

Just like the serene green on which the young
Men and women lie, the streams and red shimmers
Of our lake beyond ... I say we shall not grow old
And we shall not let the memory of our youth grow old.
I hate Mzuzu police more than ever before
For felling unarmed youths with bullets,
And for being unaware, perhaps, that as the young men
And women lie on the ridge, as they do,
And their blood soaks through the dark soil, as it does,
Then soon their blood will lend bloom to the plateau.

What wrong have the people done?

We know them by the scars we bear
Coeval midnight visitors
      parading out in uniformed footstep
      leaving claw marks on their victims.
We know them by the chain marks branded around our ankles
Dhow riders from the east trafficking in humans
      kingpins from clove farms
      gluttons of gold and elephant tusks.
Can gentleness efface marks of violence, prayer atone humiliation?
Can violence heal itself? We prefer victory to survival –
      they soured the wind: we are the whirlwind
      we'll rise and triumph, and sweep away the filth.
We know them by the scratch marks on our mothers' navels
Men who came without women, looters of the sacred
      they wreaked havoc on us in fields
      raped our sisters in slave chambers.
Our land and labor taken over for their profit, their version
Of history rings hollow, their sense of justice an insult –
      for too long they anointed themselves maker of our history
      we will now make it ourselves.

The Victim

Every day at home I watched the landlord flog his men and bellow
Curses at them: one day I saw one lad straightened up in a last groan
Of pain as he fell off the hay pile shot through the head
The landlord grinned with delight, the air tensed, my eyes watered.

As I walked through tall grass along a stream
I saw how the soil was pure; the banks still fair and green
I watched a herd stoop to pasture, their eyes glistening
And my heart throbbed faster; my spirits rose high and clear.

At the riverbanks I watched a mouse tossed downstream
And merge in the eddies still fighting, and my heart grew heavy
As he clung to a vibrating reed like a tattered flag
I saw how the current overpowered him.

Downstream I came across an abandoned rusty rifle
In the arresting silence I slowly looked around, sweating,
Then, with a deep sigh bent down, picked the heavy load,
Started climbing the hillside, back to the farm.

Shooting at students

From my balcony at Chimaliro
I could see through the haze
The cone of the hill of Mzuzu city
And the secondary school that bears its name,
The sprawling Moyale barracks
Where the northern army is based
The broadcasting station, the civic center
The high court opposite the police station
And also barely visible through the mist
The outlines of the market square
And the city stadium at Chasefu;
But, hidden from view,
I could not see the Taifa Marke Square.

Through the haze, I saw a litany of youths
Carrying protest posters too far to read –
My nephew is a student at the secondary school.
Is he up there with the others? I wondered.
No. He is a studious type, I thought.
Too conscious of his school motto:
Per studios so dares,
'Through studies we gain friends.'
I finished whatever I was doing,
Gulped the last drop of orange juice,
And dragged my notebook satchel downtown,
Noting that the label on the juice bottle said
That the squash was made from orange trees
Grafted to lemon stems and
Grown on Mazoe sandy dirt in Zimbabwe,
But this was no time for the trivial.

I passed St. John's Hospital,
My head reeling from ambulance sirens
And screeching of tires on the asphalt, and people

Every which way running towards downtown.
Perched at the edge of the Vipya plateaus
Mzuzu in spring is not like any other city:
It's a landscape of spectacular
Native beauty with hills and valleys
That stretch across the horizon,
Endowed with flowers of various hue and green
And grass of sweet fragrance.
But this was July, and the city was staggered
With wilted flower and desiccating earth.
I hurried across the bridge, veered round
To Taifa Market Square, passed the filling station,
And came face-to-face
With the throng of protesters overflowing
The dual carriageway, slowing down traffic
As they drifted downtown, some with the red-and-grey
Colors of Mzuzu secondary school;
And that is when I heard police officers, in fatigue,
Like rats at a refuse-heap when it is too wet for cats,
With their buttons held high, like rhinoceros tails,
Order their rifled marksmen
To fire at the retreating youths.
Many fell, strewn across the dual carriageway.
I saw a shirt torn off somebody's body
And a red-and-grey scarf
I recognized as my nephew's.
"Bloody hell!" I shouted to no one.
"You have killed unarmed people here! ... "
As armed men yanked me down
And wrenched the soaked scarlet scarf
Out of my hands.

Marching out on Buckingham

We are defenders of the faith, he mused on the public
Investiture of the day, the ones that sustain the empire,
We are servants of the great Queen. Harry Johnston,
Summoned by Her Majesty Queen Victoria, was to be
Conferred the Order of Saint George and Saint Michael.

And he awaited her arrival.

I want to feel her hand, the sacred royal hand beyond
Compare: the hand of the gracious Queen. Not many
Have had such luck in life. Not many. I've borne
The sword and carried the banner down
The Great Rift Valley to the sparkling points of water;

Harry Hamilton Johnston, sitting among guests
Of the queen, on a bench in Buckingham Palace
Surveyed the room; well decorated, he thought.
No! Regally decorated – splendor, power ... *sui generis*.
All round is regal dignity.

Time was ninety minutes past schedule.

Lux Britannica – illumination we perilously
Relayed *LUX IN TENEBRIS* across the dark land:
Through Tunis, Ja-Ja's Angola, Msiri, corpse-stinking
Arab dhows that trafficked in humans,
To that little country by the shimmering lake ...

Our mission was simple: to spread civilization to
The Dark Continent and its Miam-Miam savages
And stand witness for the exceptional "scepter isle,
This little world, this precious stone set in silver sea –
This England." We are the upholders of the faith...

Sir Harry Hamilton Johnston, as he'll henceforth
Be called, listened to military music, turned his gaze
to his wristwatch. Magnificent Swiss engineering,
Measure of time and labor as articles of capitalism ...
Trifles! I'm for greater things - "and the greatest is to come."

Sneers zeroed in on the future knight

The awaited hour, pinnacle of time had arrived,
Her Royal Highness, the Queen, was at hand.
The selection of banner bearers had commenced,
Reward for chivalry, presentation of insignia, induction ritual,
Conferment of knighthood ... "I command you
To rise and serve the Empire! ... "

The dubbing of the knight, time of rejoicing, great jubilation ...

The decoration ... She stretched out her hand to the full ...
True to form, Sir Harry rose from the investiture stool, gallantly. ...
The hour of chivalry, fulfillment, the raising of the sword,
Moment for rejoicing.... touch of the goddess, the great Queen,
The woman towering above all mankind... He bowed.

"We must congratulate you, Sir Harry, on your magnificent recovery.
Why, it's only recent we received reports of your escape from
Nubian savages, who, we understand, wounded you in the back.
As a great nation, our mission in Africa is clear: to bring light to
Darkness, and no heathenish act will deter us in our noble endeavor..."

Time of ritualized ceremony was over; the hour had passed.

Sir Harry hesitated for a moment, but bowed again. Of course
He'd heard about a British soldier in the Sudan who'd strayed
Into the Mahdi's path and had been stabbed in the back;
But for such to be confuse with him, and at this hour? Incredible!
Sir Harry bowed once more and marched out on Buckingham.

43

Fluttering over figs

I lingered about in the shade of the woods, soundless,
Listening to sounds of summer blossoms.
In the nearby anthill tree leaves rustled gently through
The breeze as speckled mouse birds scampered in space
Flapping their wings, rendering noon with their calls.
I, a late arrival, paused under the broad leaves of a fig tree.
I picked a sandy fig and cut into it with my teeth, silent
In the shadow of summer, letting the soft
Sweet taste of its seeds tingle the white of my teeth.
I watched golden-breasted starlings
Fight over the ripe fruits, fluttering their wings ...
After a while, I could no longer stand and stare:
There was so much else to do.

The color of pocked leaves

As the early birds brighten dawn, shadows
dispense from the brows of the hill
the sky over the ridge begins to lighten
and the colors of pocked leaves
return swiftly to their base. I'll take the air,
I thought. I will walk around the bluff
and up to the edge of the *miombo* woodland
where the grass is still green
and the mountain breeze lunges
headlong into the pass. I will look for
a pair of grizzled duikers
that frequent the undergrowth,
root out fallen *musolo* fruits,
and smear their gland secretions
on shrub stems. I will watch woodpeckers
jab at woodlice in the morning sun,
taking care not to scare them.
Still, what is up has to come down
and the bustle of morning blossoms
will descend the bluff and I'll head back
to the village at the bend of the stream,
back to a house with a cold hearth.

Where the woods begin

Mist lifted slowly from the valley
As I descended from the ridge
Breathing silently into the rising air
Listening to birdsongs.
Something was distracting me, something,
I was sure, at the edge of the woods.
I will come to it, I thought. I will come to it
And inquire further into the matter.
My initial disposition was to turn back
And have nothing further to do
In these woods, but something else
Was keeping me from getting away.
There was something about in the air,
A feeling that I have been here before,
And I was tempted to wait a little longer
To look around the woods,
For there was something
There, at the edge of the woods.
But I'll to it later, I thought.

Is there a hollow she is the shape of, I wondered.
What slips free to float across the sky like a bubble
And casts blight on the foliage?
I will come to it where the woods begin.
Whatever is out there are things
Towards which I dream.

How low the cactus bushes were,
How long has day been waiting?
If you asked me
I could not remember
What it was that had changed.
If you asked me
I could not say

Where we first met.
We probably first met
Where happiness resides,
In the silent gap of thorn bushes
That runs through the creek,
In the greenery of the small anthills
Dotting the landscape.
The wind moves through it
To trills of elephant grass,
And when I look away from the hills
Whatever it remind me of,
I'll come to it later.

Fashioning a home in the hills

There was silence in the woods
As we stepped over the boulders
And climbed to the summit.
The hills opened into a trough landscape
Lush and green miles in diameter.
There was no other place in sight,
And we were tired.
We'll settle here, my father said to us.
We'll build here and see what can be molded
Out of these boulders.
We'll live out our lives here.
With the strength we have left
We'll fashion our home from these rocks
And by our fruits people shall know us
So that in times to come
Those who venture this far will say:
They came through the hills
And, with bare hands
Turned the boulders into blossom.
But should anyone cross our path
We'll turn to our mountain gods
And spill our blood across the land.

Canopied foliage

Strong stench of canopied foliage
streamed all around us, reinforcing
after-sunset humid tropical vapors
as we wade slowly through grey grass;

The sky chimed as the slewing light
came over distant hills across the plain
striking the edge of white boulders –
hideout of the notorious city bandits;

We had decided to walk in the wood
along the boulder ridge diving shrub
from pine forestation, we stood, like fugitives,
trembling each to each in subdued spasms;

In the tall kachere bush by the anthill
birds flapped and scampered on dry twigs
making a great noise in the setting sun
and squirrels piped shrilly on the side hill;

Over the distant hillside two big black
buzzards sailed slowly round and round
their shadows slipping smoothly and quickly
ahead of them – some animal must surely

Have died in the surrounding country.
I felt an uncertainty in the air
a feeling of change and loss and
a strange sinister beginning.

All things seem circular

To a tawny-orange white-browed scrub-robin
Prominently perched onto an anthill euphorbia
In the crisp air of an autumn day, flitting
Her cocked tail, rattling in a high-pitched call
All things seem circular: rootlets, clumps
Of grass and spider webbing holstering her nest,
Stream courses, deciduous woodlands, garden
Clearings, little hills marking her territory,
Termite galleries where she probes for food,
The sky and distant ridges where the sun rises,
The horizon where migration routes merge,
Where the wind whistles through broken eggs ...

She laments for mothers no longer able to sleep
At roost, being too afraid to expose their brood,
She laments for the many who wistfully stare
From their nests, cowering down from predator birds,
She laments over circles of polluted swamps
Reeking of pesticides and putrid smell of rotting
Matter that encroach on her territory;
She bemoans the hammerhead's fate – sailing back
To its large nest she missed penetration in flight,
Blinded by a widening pall of smoke from factory
Chimneys that profits corporate bosses
But kills the grub she feeds on.

She watches cloned pesticides spread
Like grit and permeate the water sources,
Breeding sludge that infest garden beetles
Now cluttering up the countryside with shells,
Otters and water mongooses spatter blood
When they cough, waddle along in sewer stench.
When she returns to her nest, concealed

In the dense matted scrub close to the ground,
She finds it empty of its clutch. She frets about,
Fans her tail, flicks her wings, flies from tree to tree,
Scolding, rattling, flapping …
She stops, looks about, raises and lowers
Her wings, and resolves to stock up on energy
And prepare for the flight path of migration.
In the brilliant rays of the rising sun, unnoticed,
She rises like a meteor and soars to the beyond.

Peddling village gossip

My village school is a kachere tree
Around which our instructor
Gathers us for Catechism.
I am not good at memorizing
So I quit.
My village is without books
From which to memorize,
But its full of gossip and adventure.
In my village people get news
By word of mouth,
So the days I quit Catechesis
I felt happy and joyful making
The rounds, listening to old
Stories told by grandmothers.
My sister, Hlupekile, was born mute
So she does not go to school,
School being what it is,
And she takes great delight
In watching us at play in summer
When school is in recess.
We, village kids, gather by an anthill
At the edge of the village;
I like playing at the sliding,
But the slide is for older boys,
And my old brother
Makes the older boys let me play.
And what bliss!
I ride on the wooden sledge
And slide down the anthill
Charging like a buffalo,
Lifting and gliding,
Turning and twisting to
Cheers of my peers.
Hlupekile, my sister, delights

In seeing me play,
And should the older boys
Sneer at my play, I know
She knows why.

Locusts (for Tichafa)

What I like most on a January morning
Is cycling across lush fields, whistling,
Peddling gossip round villagers. Fascinated,
I trail pointed hills that stretch away into
The distance, laced with shrubs and red earth.
A flock of palm swifts dart through the air,
Scream shrilly against the blue, and swerve
Hillward, sighting a cloud of winged termites.
I let my bicycle wheel against maize stalks.
In the nearby thickets grey-headed bush shrikes
Whistle, looping from tree to tree, loeries shriek,
Clamber in a tangle over blackberries,
And fill the hills with echoes of their calls.

Beyond a small stream, west, a whizz of wings
Mob the horizon as myriads of alien grasshoppers
Swarm the veld, grisly glistening green, dreadfully
Eclipsing the sun dark. Shouts, drumbeats, and
Clanging of pots resound from all over the ridges
As farmers come out to clobber the rapacious visitors
With hoes and axe handles, trying to save their crops.
Within minutes the land is stripped bare and grey:
Where before bees droned in brush and green
Now stumps and boulders lie naked and ugly,
Where robins had flustered into song
Now silence echoes hushed from the hills.
I picked my bicycle and pushed into the next village
To wails of farmers choked over pungent ordure.

*ordure: excrement .

The Kamilaza stream

In the place where I was born
the Kamilaza stream no longer unrolls
placid as a bridle path between hills,
zebu cattle dotting its grazing banks.
I used to ride my bicycle along the ridge
down to Embangweni school
swerving and breaking
on the zig-zag path that winds down the hills
bracing against the wind
pursued by pebbles uprooted from the wheel path.
On my way back
on a warm summer afternoon
I would stop by a group of
people at Thoza junction playing *bawu*,
recent returnees from migrant labor abroad,
there being no employment opportunities
on the ridge. Seeing me approach
they would pause from their game,
only briefly, note my crazy
acrobatics on wheels
and shake their heads.
I had time for everything – sometimes
I would dismount from my bike
to tell stories embellished
from my day at school.
But one day agents from some
international donors arrived
and, in the name of wealth
creation and free market economy,
earmarked Thoza for induction into
the global economy.
They brought bulldozers
and ploughed the ridge,
seeding it with tobacco for export.

They felled trees and saturated
the Kamilaza watershed with pesticides,
draining the ridge of its fauna and stories ...
I still stop by Thoza junction in summer
to trade old tales with aging *bawu* players
who, in their stupor of despair,
still call me by name.
I have recently been introduced to
laid-off workers from the project, there being
a glut of tobacco on the global market,
and there still being no employment on the ridge.
I have dreamt of banding them together
into a cooperative to restore the Kamilaza basin
to lush, pesticide-free corn, soya bean,
and pumpkin fields that will transform Thoza
into an ox-drawn food trough bulging with produce...
At moments like this
I remember each of these things
and do not much care if they are true:
the dried-up Kamilaza stream,
in its wind-swept meander, its banks desiccated,
emptied of its unrolling images of the past
is enough to make my story.

The new well

They drilled a hole in the sand in the middle of my village,
A borehole donated by some non-governmental organization
To ease water shortage and reduce water-borne diseases, they said,
Such as diarrhea, amoebic dysentery, and scabies, and the like.

No water was found, and a mob of irate villagers ripped the steel
Pipes off to make hoes. Every afternoon, after grazing,
Village boys tether their goats around the new well to play
And marvel at the gaping hole in the middle of the village.

One day a kid strayed from its nanny goat, nibbling millet husks
Left by some farmer's wife at the edge of the gaping hole.
Suddenly the kid slipped and fell to the bottom of the shaft.
The children told me that such incidents happen all the time,
Ever since donors sunk the hole in the middle of the village.

See the children play

I like to see the children play on the village sand
Their bodies shiny, grayed with particles of dust
As they tumble and sprawl in dirt, unperturbed,
Their little legs stamping all over the place,
Their eyes sparkling in the morning sun
Their teeth splendid in laughter
Their voices shrills of pure joy
Making the whole day one long game.

The children at school

Mangisani, soccer player, maneuvers, dribbles, twists and
Turns, unhappy and restless when he finds nothing else to do,
Enjoys reggae music, frolics and helps in the kitchen, asks
Few questions in class, I am told, and his grades show.

Chimwemwe, a friendly joyful fellow, visitor's favorite;
Fixes bicycles, mows the yard, and the palms of his hands show.
On summer days, pleasant, cheerful, and arduous about work,
Brooks no nonsense from his coach and is now without a team.

Tichafa, alert, sharp as a razor blade, a fine rap fun, but
He's a mind of his own. He asks many questions, rarely
Waits for answer, asks why children in Africa starve?
Devoted to helping disadvantaged artists on the continent.

Leya, vivacious, applied late for the basketball team and was
Left out. Knowing it would annoy others, watches television
Non-stop. Homesick, like me, she views old photographs of
Departed aunts and uncles with vague recollections only.

Tamaliyapo, 'the ultimate!' she wrote on her wall.
What I like best is to see her play in the sun, her body
Clay-covered, her eyes sparkling, her elated voice a shrill
Of great delight, her little legs jumping all over me,
Making the day a joy of life. I lean back, grateful to bask
In the warm glow of these precious gifts, the children.

A daughter's questions

Why should night follow day, you ask.
Why should life be followed by death?
Why is the east always red at sunrise? Etc.
Oh, sweet innocent mind!

Green comes with the shine of an absolute day
When the rays of the sun wander in the supple of plants –
Here violets and lilies, there mahogany and sycamore,
Life is all things luminous that delight us in their fullness.

Things you ask are what show us the lengthening day
Through which life and joy; death and sadness pass. I lost
My dear parents recently, dear child, so I come with no
Answers, for sadness always overwhelms me.

Our story

Please hear me out, for I speak plainly:
If you leave now, you deny me
If you return, you will arouse me, for
We are lovers of a different kind, you and I,
We are nature's mystery –
As water finds her own level
So too will life protect its own.
We'll cover ourselves with leaves of the wild
For trees do not swing into sneers,
Leaves do not break into laughter
And the wind, however widely it blows,
Does not divulge secrets.
Our love, bathed in the mystic rites
And ceremonies of Thoza,
Shall survive our departure
And flourish among these sunny hills
Long after we are gone.
Farmers and herds' boys
Will tell the story of our love,
Pools and rapids will echo the rapture of
Our existence, and, as a prelude
To the new moon, songbirds
Will liven the evening light
With sweet melodies of the season …
Long shall Thoza youths gaze
At the midnight sky and marvel
At the star-spangled Milk Way
Sparkling like a meteor, my love,
Spurred on by your splendor.

Writing on sand

Joel Ndhlovu was our teacher's name: he was a stickler
And held his class underneath a *kachere* tree where we,
His pupils, daily scoured the schoolyard for a patch of sand
To level with our palms into a writing slate on which
To do our class work – unless, of course, the rains beat us to it
And wiped out clean all our hard day's labor!
During arithmetic, we wrote answers in the sand with our fingertips,
Drew numbers with addition or multiplication signs
Sometimes the sand would spill over the line and blur the answer.
Our teacher, Mr. Joel Ndhlovu, would stoop low
To grade the answers, and scuff over the sand-slate when he was done.
We smoothed out the sand with the palm of our hands all over again,
Arranging and rearranging the grains of sand for the next exercise;
The same was true when it came to unscrambling the alphabet:
We first traced our names in the sand, as temporal as it was.
The name Qita, with a click, was changed to Peter with a stop –
Stops being more familiar to the ear of the missionary Scotsman
Who occasionally visited our school, and every time you said your name
Teacher Ndhlovu would jump up and say: "Write it down! Write it down"
Holding his stick over your head. And woe betide anyone
Who failed to comply with his instructions!
Like recruits to a drill surgeon, we would all snap back to our sand patches
And, like the new recruits, we all knew what to do: *write it down*!
Such, then, was the routine at Thoza School when I was young. At home
My grandmother would often times, with her stick, dodder about
The village yard, waiting for my return from school.

The delicacy of the hills

I'm a fine young man; I was born in a spot
In northern Malawi they call it Thoza
My village arranged on a ridge, my house
Built of wattle and rafter. On market days I sell
Honey, game meat; pigeon peas; fried termites; mushroom,
And dried vegetables wrapped in *musuku* leaves.
On Sunday I sell secondhand clothes to farmers' wives
That flock to my stalls for flea market bargains.

I scour through the scrubby hillsides on Friday,
Tracking bee-eaters hunting for honey, setting traps
To catch deer, duiker and guinea fowl, and I thatch
The small huts on ant heaps to ensnare flying termites,
The delicacy of Thoza! My wife fries the termites
With a secret seasoning and spreads them out on reed mats,
The finest delicacy you will find in these hills.
But the best is the dried mushroom that only my aunt
Makes. If cooked with local vinegar and groundnut sauce,
It would do you good to taste a sampling at her stall.

At the show grounds on Saturday, I make quite a spectacle,
Visitors flock to my stall drooling, looking for a bargain
Their eyes dazzled by the splendor of my wares
Spread out at the corner. After a sampling of game
Meats and fried termites, self-deceiving talkers ask
"Who makes these, the finest delicacies in the hills?"

The carpenter

His grandfather cut wood for a living, so did his father. He makes
And repairs woods, knows the names of trees from which hardwood
Timber is made: *m'mbawa, mnyezane, mukuyu, chiyele, sendelela,*
Mlombwa, Et cetera. He has an assemblage of tools: mallet, coping saw,
Adze, clamps, drawknife, grooving plane, and knows also the various
Home improvements uses of woods in a good carpentry
Shop: *Mukuyu* is for mortar making; *mnyezane* for
Cupboard; *chiyele* for door panels; *m'mbawa* for small accessories;
And bed frames, a communal sharing of the sanctity of life, are made from
mlombwa. He planes wood pieces and joins them together into complex
Shapes of desks, shelves, tables, chairs, ox cart, pestles, hoe handles,
And many more, according to the season, needs, and tastes of his clients.
To ensure his wares are tough and flexible, he only uses stitch and glue
To enhance wood appearance and boost bridle, dovetail, and tongue and
Grove joints. To treat the wood, he uses veneer, glue, varnish and color
Stains, depending on the grain of the wood and texture – it is in the family
For his grandfather was a carpenter, as was his father,
And he excels in sawing the wood, curving groves
And making wood designs to the desires of his clients.
His trade is cutting through blocks of wood to make furniture
Making shiny surfaces with varnish and polish for decorations –
For every household seeks him out to decorate their homes.
He makes sweet fruits out of block wood and saw shavings –
For he is a workman who repairs the woods, as his father did.
I wonder what they would say, who hold these woods sacred,
As progenitors, as their totemic emblems, about a dynasty of carpenters
That fells reserved trees, planes them into wood pieces,
And joins them together into complete shapes for profit?

The sawyers of Thoza

There is something about big trees I cannot remember.
Behind our village there was an enormous deciduous tree
Centuries old by any measure, I am sure. One day, two men
With a two-handled crosscutting saw arrived, cut the tree down,
And, with a bucking saw, sawed off the big tree into logs.
They constructed a sturdy sawhorse of narrow plank scaffolding
On which they rolled up the logs, one by one,
And hoisted a two handled whipsaw eight feet above ground.
One sawyer balanced on the plank trestles holding one end
Of the saw, the other stood on the ground below the log,
Holding the other end. Together, alternating one after the other,
Up and down, the sawyers pulled the sharp-toothed
Edge of the two-man saw right through the logs,
Turning the wood into planks, and spraying the ground
With shavings and a haze of sawdust.
The top sawyer balanced the log and guided the long saw
Along a charcoal line to maintain even thickness of the board
And to keep the cuts straight or curved as required.
If the kerf began to close, which can cause the saw to bind,
Wedges were inserted to keep it open and reduce friction.
Work was hard, but the sawyers were proud of their trade
And timber was what was in demand – what they needed to sell
To put food on the table and pay for their children's schooling.
They were at it all day, and the next, and next ...
Occasionally they would stop to wipe off sweat from their foreheads
And catch back their breaths, but otherwise they were at it all day.
Nobody fell off the scaffoldings, but one day
After the two sawyers had hoisted a *muwula* log onto the sawhorse
The ground man tripped on an old tree stump as he reached
For his end of the saw handle and slumped into the shavings,
And the big saw slipped from its hold and fell on his foot
Severely damaging his big toe. Bearing several old scars already,
It didn't bleed so much but needed six stitches at the local clinic.
Now a new craze for plastic furniture imported from abroad

Has invaded the market and hardwood lumber is no longer in demand;
The scaffolding at the old sawhorse has been cut up and sold to
A new forest resort facility, and turned into wood cladding
Gateposts against inspiring lush gardens of imported flora.
The ground sawyer, still with a limp, has not spent another day
With old trees, and now patronizes the facility, peddling
His illicit wares to tourists, his children still not in school.

Kerf - the width of a saw cut (Anglo-Saxon word related the word 'carve')

You are no friend of mine

Cheers of intoxicated revelers gulping pints of beer,
Rumba music, whistles of block party gatecrashers
We stagger into each other and snap into invective.

We do not pause to reflect on the rowdy company,
But know here is no time for niceties and palaver for
We do not know each other at all.

When dawn knocks and chases away the night
We do not pause and say farewell, but quietly
Slip away into our dark spots and daily routine.

We peer deep into the horizon for handclaps
And call up fragments of memories, but none
Is in sight, for you are no friend of mine.

Zilani

He left us shocked and deeply grieved.
Being last of three brothers,
Fourth in the line of six siblings,
He was my dear friend and brother.
He was a favorite son of our clan.
He caught us unawares, departing so early
Like someone who arrives late at a party,
Says he cannot stay
And leaves without notice.

Twirl of life

We walk briskly along, our breath twirling in the cold air.
Shine or rain, we assume things are what they should be
We sit and ponder long how the sun will come out tomorrow
And what the weather forecasters will say.
From the shards that encircle the hearth and give us
Warmth, we fill our minds with castles fit for a Zulu chief
As we twirl slowly across towards the exit.

The travails of leaving

Is it true that you are leaving, she asked?
Yes, I said.
I hardly knew her, but there was such
A distressed tone in her voice;
He is so upset. My son, I mean.
To hear you are leaving.
I met her son a month ago, playing
Skip in the yard of our apartment
And I stopped by to say hello,
Conscious of the risk of
Being misunderstood.
He told me about his school
And the subjects he is taking,
And I told him about myself.
He looked lonely. I sat down
And read him a story about
The hare and tortoise
From the book I was carrying.
He expressed great interest in the story,
 And I told him he could keep the book
And read the other stories.
Then I took him to his mother
And introduced myself.
He'll be ten tomorrow, she said.
He's had no father figure – his father
Being on death row.
I'm sorry to hear that, I said.
No, no, no. She said. It's all right.
Why do you have to leave so soon, she asked.
We have just started knowing you.
The economy being the way
It is now; I said I couldn't pay rent,
And I am out of work.
It's a sad situation, isn't it, she said?

We read in the papers – people being out of work,
Forced out of their homes.
There was a look of sorrow on her face
And I didn't know what to think.
You see; I like to arrive at a place unnoticed
And leave without fanfare.
I can never be a neighborhood watch
And accost people considered intruders.
I like coming into a place, live there
For a while, and then depart;
Fade back into where I came from.
My presence counts for nothing, really,
And there was no complication – until now,
With this lady, whose name I don't know,
Who was distraught at my leaving,
And whose fatherless child was now upset.
She is pretty, and has a wonderful son
But what was it about her
That moved her so totally about
A non-event?
This poem is for her.

Loneliness

In the evenings
she'd walk alone
through the woods,
they said she suffered
from the widow disease
that metastasizes with age;

And that's how
she was introduced
to Mr. Loneliness
who shook her hand
as they sat down to chat,
basking in smoldering embers;

Between pauses
they measured their lives
in cups of warmed spice tea
recounting tales of long ago,
stories of wonder, past glories,
and lost chances.

Why the old woman limps

Do you know why the old woman sings?
She is sixty years old with six grandchildren to look after
While her sons and their wives are gone south to dig gold.
Each day she milks the goat, sells the milk to buy soap,
Feeds and washes the children, and tethers the goat.
In the evening she tells all stories of old at the fireside:
I know why the old woman sings.

Do you know when the old woman sleeps?
She rests with the dark, at night she thinks of
Tomorrow: she's to feed the children and graze the goat,
She's to weed the garden, water the seedling beans,
The thatch has to be mended, the barnyard cleared,
Maize pounded, chaff winnowed, millet ground, fire lit …
I do not know when the old woman sleeps.

Do you know why the old woman limps?
She goes to fetch water in the morning
            and the well is five miles away,
Goes to fetch firewood with her axe
            and the forest is five miles the other way,
Goes to the fields to look for pumpkin leaves
            leaving the goat tethered to the well tree
And hurries home to the children to cook:
I know why the old woman limps.

Witnessing the setting sun

I call upon the evening to commence,
The moon and stars to rise brightly
In the silvery sky that envelopes the earth
The village elders to beat the big drums
The young initiates to take to the arena…

But isn't it a little late now? The young men having
Been enlisted into migrant work by recruitment
Bureaus, maids lured by glittering city lights
And many members of the generation forced
Into exile, the youthful evening will not come.

The sky will darken red with the setting sun
The earth overcast with thick thunderclouds
Light from stars will obliterate the crescent moonlight
Embers from bonfires will sputter into a dim glow
And the village will lapse back to its graying stupor.

My father, sitting on the verandah, silvery and grey,
Will scan the crescent for signs of the solstice,
Will listen for footsteps of initiates on the dry earth.
And although the big drums will be tightly tuned
The dance arena will remain silent.

Vuso

We carried the casket in a jeep
Six feet of wood draped with flowers
Forty years of youth and vitality
Crashed into the metal entanglement
On a lonely road at Liwonde,
Years of friendship ended on a somber journey.
There were people everywhere, wailing
And bombarding heaven with questions
On a tender life, taken away so young.

We passed Lilongwe after dark
Huddled together in the back of a jeep
Trying to reach Ephangweni before dawn,
Our emotions measured by their closeness
To the death of our friend, strapped into a casket.
The women sung, barely droning out our tears.
We stopped at Kasungu to refuel
And arrived at Jenda junction after midnight
Taking cares not to awaken sleeping street vendors
By our wails and protests at a life taken so young.

We drove through Chafi*si*, winding and twisting
Across the Rukuru River, and slowly glided to Baleni
In bright moonlight amidst trills of nightingales
And wails of awakened villagers blaming God for
Vuso's death. When we reached Ephangweni
We could hear miles around wails of people
Crying, pounding their chests, asking God
What sin they had committed to be so punished.
We sifted the dust from the hearse, that shiny
Woody remains of my dear, childhood friend.

Then, at sunrise, after fires had been set for shivering
Hearse bearers, women burst into Ngoni songs of old,

As is the tradition, and you could hear the melodies
Whichever way you turned. It was touching, the women
Asking God in *ChiNgoni*, why a man so young
Had to be taken before his time. There was no sound
Of twittering birds just then, the wind being against them,
And the wailing and singing of shocked villagers
Being louder: It was a sad day, if you must know.

In the middle of it all, people paused, pointed heavenward
Mumbling to themselves about the anger in their bellies
For a life cut short. For you who must know, they said,
For you, the uncertain destination, the end,
What is the purpose of birth if death awaits us so?
I decided I wasn't going to hear out
The priest who had known Vuso from youth,
Nor the elders who sung Vuso's eulogies in *chiNgoni*
Nor the chiefs who were advocating for re-dedication
And valor – I wasn't going to listen to anyone
Unless they could explain to me, point by point,
Why so beautiful a life had to be taken away so young?
If Vuso's mother, sobbing profusely, heaving with deep
Grief, asked why her son, so young, now lies
On a cold bed of sand in the creek, what would the priest
Say to her? Would he say go and ask God in heaven?
Or would he turn away like a cloistered sister
And pry between curtains of mourners?

The artist who wouldn't dance (for Chinua Achebe)

He stood at the edge of the auditorium platform, pensive,
And there was no one else on stage. The most renowned
Singer and songwriter on the African continent had been
Invited, for a fee, to sing before a special audience
At the world famous institute of the performing arts
Where only the world's best can expect an invitation
(The rest send in their resumes).
The famous artist was about to step up to the podium
When an embarrassingly agitated official told him
About a regrettable typing error in the invitation letter:
The 'special audience' referenced was deaf, not sight impaled!
Therefore, he said with an imploring glance, the welcoming
Committee was requesting if the honored guest could perform
A tribal dance instead, the movements of which the audience
Can watch and appreciate, rather than sing a song
Whose melodies they cannot hear. Cognizant of
The inconvenience caused, he said in a lowed voice,
The committee is willing to review the fee. Having assured
The official that he would give his response directly to the
Waiting audience the murmur in the auditorium quieted
Down a bit when he stepped forward, stood for a moment
At the lectern, and then drew himself up to the microphone.
An eerie quietness descended in the room. "Stop
Daydreaming," he said, softly, looking at the committee.
"I am not a dancer, and I will not dance!" And he broke into
The most beautiful melody ever performed in the auditorium.

A patched heart

Since a team of doctors inserted
Angioplasty into my left
Anterior descending to ease
Blockage I have learned to slow
Down in my routine. I saw
The whole operation on screen
And thought "it's dark in there."
But the doctors said,
With a little dieting and exercises
I should be just fine.
To reduce cholesterol, they advised,
Take statin, and stay away
From red meats, yolk, liver, butter,
And ice creams. If kept within
These strictures, they said,
The heart will survive,
Shivers kept at bay,
And stamina will improve.
Thus with a punctured heart
I have learned to love life,
My children, my family,
And friends who taught me
What it is to love and be loved;
And that, at the end of day,
No work should be left undone.

On the battlefield

On the battlefield, robots
and unmanned predator planes
won't even care who wins
definition of heroes and valor
being obsolete.
The victor, in seismic rubble,
will brittle at his post, debris,
a smoldering piece of flint
indistinguishable from
the vanquished.

When the storms come

In time
       the lake will surge
       tossing pots
       gullying the soil
       in mid-current red showers

I am the blank between the colors
I am the one that foresees the end

In time
       the storm will come
       flooding the shores
       plateau and mountains will crumble
       to level in tribal conflagrations

I am the interspace between tongues
I am the one that foresees the end

In time
       the sea will wash away the stain
       leaving the gash putrified
       and beyond cleansing

I am the blank between the colors
       the interspace between tongues
       the one who foresees the end.

Rumors of war

Everywhere there are tremors of war, science
And technology mounded around military hardware,
Germ spores stockpiled into shimmers of war, ships,
Submarines, surface to air missiles, rocket launchers,
Aircraft carriers, drones, etc., modeled and molded again
For war, armies, commandoes, special forces, assassins,
Spies and interrogators trained and trained again
For war, and the media, to benefit the war industrial
Complex is busy advancing the virtues of war.

Meanwhile, in the third world millions of children
Die of hunger and curable diseases. In the countryside
Cornfields are dry; children cower in shades, too weak
To play, their bellies bloated, their mothers emaciated
They pull up roots of wild berries, scavenging for food.
Despite frequent epidemics and natural disasters
Arising from global warming, there are no stockpiles
Of food and medicines, farmers are not trained,
And weather technologies are not remolded.

When war breaks out, bombs from unmanned aircrafts
Will explode, cruise missiles from submarines launched
And a ball of fire will sear the earth,
A mushroom cloud will rise into the atmosphere
Casting ensigns of chill on the countryside.
Men, women, and children will run every which way,
Coughing their lungs out, holding their eyeballs,
Their hair falling out in black flakes, their eardrums burst,
Hastened by the aftershock of war. North and south,
Haves and have-nots, there will be no survivor.

Cave painting

We assemble here today
beside these stalactites
with quills dipped into horn ochre
to etch on these granite walls
stroke by stroke,
in subtle shades of line definitions,
the history of our people.
In coats of paint,
in solid coloring mixed with oil,
we'll curve curved temple portals
to our sacred past
to show that our forefathers
died not in vain.
In remembrance of our past
I say to you, therefore,
let's inscribe on these rocks
in monochrome impulses
strokes by stroke,
the deeds of our people
so that wind and migratory birds
relay to the future
news of their existence.

But should absence of wind
or changes in the seasons
restrain the swallows
and alter the course of migration
we desire that, in a day-less time,
our people's names
and their achievements
carved on these rocks
may not perish
but shine like stars, a beacon
for whoever ventures this far.

Flashing debris – fall of an overambitious person

What comes down has been up,
To alter the old adage,
Oh the galaxy!
The firmament stands firm,
Constellations go cold
When overarching ambition
Carries a rising star too far
Above his order
Until he falters, and falls
Hurtling through space in tailed fragments,
Whizzing, flaking into a thousand sparkles,
Flare, splendor,
Tumble of flashing debris that fleetingly
Lights up the night.
And it's bliss to be awake
Under the tropical sky
On a night of shooting stars!

****

Forever grateful (for Tamaliyapo)

Every evening I would read her stories
Of the hare and the tortoise, or the hawk and the kite
And when she tires and yawns, I would tuck her
Away in her bed, gently, fragile gift, the ultimate,
Last and final, the most precious being ...
Her face a solace to me at my age,
Her life a blissful story of spring
Her presence a keen reminder that whatever
The future holds for me has not come to pass.
Tomorrow she will go bike riding again
Into the open countryside, chasing butterflies
While I sit back apprehensive about the bumpy road ahead
And the scar on her chin is a reminder
That so much is at stake before a storm.
Her poise on the bike, her dexterity
Reminds me so much of my late mother -
Her rough graceful hands when weaving baskets,
Her reassuring embraces when the weather turns stormy.
A miracle it is indeed to see a young tree
Blossoming on the blessings of the old one.
I am forever grateful for her arrival.

Where did the eland go?

I drove down the slight slope, past *Chasefu* township,
Veered downtown, and then out to the city limits.
I drove for a long time before my daughter
Asked me the meaning of the names of places
We were passing through.
"Where do I start," I said, playfully.
"Where we started," she said. "What does *Chasefu* mean?
"Eland," I said, quickly. "That was easy. It means
Eland: the largest savannah and plains antelope."
"I've never seen an eland," she said.
"Where did the name come from?"
"Some time ago," I said, "the eland was native to these parts,
And fed on shrub-like bushes. But that was a long time ago"

The eland became the theme song of my life when I was young
But such animals being gone, I did not know what else to tell her.
I imagined a long time ago herds of elands, zebras, wild hogs,
And graceful gazelles bugling fain calls through *miombo* woodlands.
"They are all gone now," I said, slowly, feeling sad.
"Shot by poachers. Some driven away by the frequent dry spells,
And some poisoned by herbicides in water holes."

I thought: the rest probably migrated west to the Luangwa
Wetlands where there is another town with a similar name,
But I wasn't sure. "All gone," I said again.
"Only their names remain, infused into the local lore."
"So what about tomorrow, dad, when the rains come back?
Will the elands return?"
I had no answer.

I imagined fenced wild game ranches in America, and
Army marksmen shooting at captured elands for sport.
I imagined African commercial farmers hacking down trees
For their estates, their tractors purposefully, like death,

Ripping apart elands' resting shades and browsing woodlands. Tamaliyapo fell quiet. She asked no further questions.

I want to be all things to you

I want to be with you
Like a grafted branch;
I want to be your dark rind
Close to the bark.
When the wind blows
And locks you in
I want to be your anchor
So you are not restless.
I want to be your taproot
Your fountain in the drought
Your lute I will be
To voice your deepest thought
I want to be all things to you
And you to be my wife,
But go ahead, spit in my face!
One day you'll be mine.

The luster of your skin

Your eyes are like rays of the sun at daybreak,
Their amused twinkle diamond crystals in the dewdrop.
Your skin a basketful of wild berries in season
Its beauty the color of rain against the green
And I, your sole worshipper, poise in supplication.

Only with the smell of lilies in the field can I love you
Only with flowers everywhere, among the swirl of rivulets,
The cooing of doves in the rain-soaked green forest,
Only against sounds of cicadas in the trees, can I love you
And truly call you my own, only in Thoza.

If freedom prevails, we shall not grow old, you and I;
At a new sunrise, you will stand tall among the folks of Thoza
And people will say: we have seen her some place else -
Look at the diamonds in her eyes, like rays at daybreak
The luster of her skin, like flowers in the field.

Tumbling over the rocks

I remember how the rain taps your shoulders
how rivulets converge down your groove
rumbling in their slumberous caresses.
I think of you every day, anxious
to once again touch your tropical ways
frolic about your river banks, free like the zebra,
watch starlings strut among wild berries. ...

With a scarf draped over your left shoulder
your greenery against the blue sarong
your undulating curves shaking in prattle
as furtive easterly winds roll headlong
over plateaus and tumble into rapids,
you fold your elbows around your breasts
your whispers descending into low tones. ...

It is winter here in Columbus, Ohio –
thirty degrees below zero with the wind shear.
I run the air conditioner to warm the scarlet-crested
canary my son brought from the mall.
The cold sneaks through a crack in the wall, my love,
reminding me how much I miss your warm embrace.
When turbulent weather begins to thaw out,
I'll light a candle for those who will not survive the storm,
and burn an old anger in me for having left you for exile.

Embers of love (for nachi)

Like sauntering in spring blossom
Let the lute you play, my love,
Summon us, unhurried, leisurely
To the chamber of love,
It is the hour we need not speak.
Let the night join us, hold us together,
Tenderly rock us to sleep,
Until fog lifts from the ridge,
Vague mist of dawn...

We huddle together in our frolic
Your hands within my hands as deeds
My tongue tingling your inner ears
Singing into them a zither tune, my love,
Mute, our arms close, eyes widened,
Your dreadlocked hair a bouncing forest …
What else can a mortal desire?

We stir against the morning breeze
Singing a rhythm unsung, my love,
Infinite in the cycle of time,
And the hills and streams
Roll around and over us forever.
Your shoulders roll, your hips sway
Side to side as you stretch your legs
And I stand erect, my love,
My eyes closed into a thought.
I walk across the room, my love, and
Look outside the window for words to
Lift me from the misty past.
Frosty chills clear from the creek,
Morning rays lean on the thatch,
Touch the edges of the room
Girdled about by streaks of bird songs

Rekindling my desire for you.

In a land divided by itself, in a place tinged
With branding marks of ethnicity, in a space
Situated by the power of your beauty
I wonder what tomorrow brings, my love.
We must withstand the roar of thunder
And not yield to the rain, however soft its
Touch, however arousing its lure.
What hope do we have, my love?

Rustled into awakening by a strutting cockerel,
We must not surrender in fear of darkness,
But rise to the hopeful rays of the sun.
We must not sink back to solitude of pain,
Or stay indoors as others have done.
We must not detach ourselves from things
We are attached to, but stand in the bright
Sun, my love, and be marked by its light.
How else can I tell it's you I dream of?

Song at daybreak

By daybreak they both thought they were gods
And wanted it to last.
How long could it last? They wondered.
They turned their faces to the wall
And shut their eyes.

They had been like that all night, inseparable,
Oblivious to all, huddled together in their grass
Thatched house, rolling on the mat, thrusting
Into frenzied moans screened by coos of
Cockerels flapping their wings to herald dawn,
Erasing time by the minute.

They lay there, snuggled in their little house,
Stretched out on a mat among a tangle of
Clothes. They thought themselves
The finest couple in the area, and in low
Tones they hummed to each other
A beautiful local lilt, the pitch
Rising higher with each repetition.

To this day, their story is told throughout
The ridges: 'Wema and NyaLongwe's son,'
Was all the gossip you heard, two youths
Immortalized in song. Now they are
Truly forever, the lyrics say.

The sun will rise, and the wind will rise, and
The two will coalesce in space. And the whole
Story will be repeated, over again and again.

The finest moment of the night

As dawn breaks red on the east, a cockcrow
From atop a wattle coop disturbs my slumbers.
A cat, invisible as the dark, lies silent in the barnyard,
Cicadas chirp away in the grey light of an almost
Imperceptible fog that unveils outlines of an anthill
Lying dimly in the reddish earth beyond. This, I know,
Sluggishly, between being awake and asleep,
Is the finest moment of the night – until I am jolted
Into full awakening by the tampan tick, suckling my blood!
Bright-red splashes define faint clouds as the countryside
Bursts into a bustle of women shrieking with laughter
Jostling with each other at the village well
And heard boys whistling their herd to pasture.

The encounter at Thoza junction

I stopped by at Thoza junction to hike a ride to the city,
There were no bus services through the hills on that day.
A voluptuous lady in her forties, with her companion
Came down from the hills. I noticed that her skin
Was the color of the soil: reddish brown, her eyes bright
And sparkling. She reminded me of something from the past,
Something I could not put my fingers on, a spot of
Bother with these hills, long ago.
I thought of Tasiyana, the girl
I should have married, that long ago. ...
A dusty pickup truck with limited space,
Stopped by to pick up passengers.
As people jostled for space, I stepped aside
And soon the van drove off, leaving me standing there.
As the truck sped away, I saw the buxom lady look back
On me, her hair ruffled by the wind.
She hesitated a little, and waved her hand.
Soon the truck and its contents went over the hill
And disappeared. And I, unsure still,
Retraced my footsteps, back to the village.
What is it between us? I said to myself.
I tried to remember what it was I had lost,
Something to be remembered, to come back to,
But it must have happened a long time ago,
Before this life began, something I don't remember.
I wish I were somewhere else, I thought.
Some place far from here, where lovebirds are extinct.
I noticed there were shards on the ground
Scattered where the women were jostling for space.
I should remember to clean up, I thought,
For there will be debris.

A touch of light

In truth, we both wanted it to last,
Laid up against each other
Erasing each minute with each minute.
How I wanted to possess her,
Stop the erasing minutes,
But she slipped away, saying
She had errands to run.

Shards of her slippage caught me unawares.
I kept after her like sunlight,
Lingered long, unwavering.
It's not what you think, she said, tapering off
Like blurred footprints on a windy day.
Now it will be forever, I thought,
Like kingdom of heaven.
Will you love me forever?
I hollered, at her receding shadow.

I could see, faintly, that she'd stopped
And turned her back on me.
She shut her eyes, her face
Turned to the evening wind.
I knew then what I know now:
She would not be the end
Towards which I was tending.
I knew also that although tomorrow
The sun would rise and I would rise
And her eyes - oh those crystal balls –
Would shine, the distance between us,
The cleft would not close.

At daybreak, everything clattered,
The long chase came to an end.
Sunbirds of various plumages,
Each making its own calls, broke into
Sweet melodies of dawn, a yearning
For her the light couldn't quench.

Something else

You see her everywhere,
Her eyes cloudy from smoke
Her skin tempered by heath fire.
Everyday she bakes, grills, broils,
And sits at the kitchen table
Until dusk comes over her
Not able to let her guard down
And let her body rest.
Along with the rest of the things,
She wants to be elsewhere
Where she can slip through the veil
Of eternity, mend her thatch,
Keep her house airy and dry,
Perform her garden chores,
Tend to her grandchildren,
And change into something
That is not something else.

Tasiyana – the return

You returned at the festive season of the hills
When farmers celebrate the ripening fruit harvest,
Radiant with your shell-blue necklace beads;

The hills lay hazy, as if from bush fires set by honey
Hunters, fanned, no doubt, by news of your return.
When the *ncwala* revelers started dancing, you coyly
Stepped into the arena, and villagers held their breath;

And then you broke into solo – melodious was
Your song, passionate ardor your voice as
It curled and reverberated into the night air;

There was a cry of joy and bewilderment, for none
Could match the perfection of your feet, the suppleness
With which your body flowed in the evening air. Yet,
Tension rose in my heart for we had parted too long.

* Ngoni first fruit celebrations

Waiting for you

The orange light of dawn,
Reflected morning dew
Doused our faces,
Stripped all colors from ochre-painted walls
Jutting into space like crops of rock.

We watched sunbirds break the quiet of morning,
And against the same fire-red backdrop of dawn
I wanted to feel the long curves of your body,
Your hands wrapped around mine,

Your sweet whispers soothing the rough edges
Of my mind with, erasing all doubts of your love.
And here, if I thought it would make you smile,
I would point out our shadow against the wall,

Point out that fullest side of the moon
That changes the tide, our dark companion
That'll never walk away from us. Yearning for you,
I intend to live fully by it.

Rhythms of the ridges

When you return to the ridges
A true gift of the seasons
Your name will rise again
Like a meteor
And Thoza will once again, as before,
Hear stories of your stunning beauty.
People will gaze in rapture
When you step into the village arena
At the dance festivals,
Your eyes glowing against the bonfires,
Your sheen an excited flash,
Your voice chanted thrills re-echoing
From hill to hill
Luring villagers to the drum music.
This indeed is the season
When lovers greet their loved ones
With gifts of flowers and necklaces
Of white beads;
And people will wonder
At your suppleness, your poise, your shine.
She has not rusted with age, they'll say.
She hasn't dimmed with the blight of the seasons.

Wema's return to the hills

When Wema returned to Thoza at season's end
The ridges were festive with carnivals of the first fruit.
Still, every which way, people turned and noticed,
Even trees leaves seemed to whisper
Their leaves swaying as they reached for the sun,
Nightjars muttered their night songs as if to break a spell
Lizards slithered round tree trunks and peeped
Children playing moon games stopped and turned,
Toddlers trailed along behind their mothers
And soon people's feet quickened, their breaths steamed,
And the village chatter fell silent. When people saw
That she was the presumptive beauty
That I sing about they were filled with wonder
For love, although deemed common,
Is a rare occurrence on the sidewalk of life.
I was indeed greatly indebted to her for her return,
For, except in moments of whisper,
It was the youthful romance that evoked memories
Of awe in me, with nostalgia scarcely remembered.

The dancer

To the rhythm of drums, your voice; to chirrups of nightjars,
Your luminous body unbound, pacing in undulations.
Is that her soul that voice? People will say.
All over the villages, women will pause from their daily chores
And crouch over their hearths to listen to your melodious voice
Resonating like a flock of birds on a range, stirring villagers into frenzy

What am I to do but let my gaze linger a little longer
On the gait of your poise, the fullness of your passion.
The outpour of your voice, water soft, like flowers in the field,
Lyrical, like waves cutting up the plateau, will rise in the evening air
Turning laments of unsatisfied love, unfulfilled mortal happiness,
Into nostalgia of the season's fragrance of lilies in bloom

In the bright sun, my love, lily calyxes open into delicate broad colors
That quiver free in the air, yet wilt and die when the sun goes down –
Sunless-ness kills them! Love ends like a village path marked 'no outlet'
What is the use crying when tears fade into salt crystals on the cheek?
Unlike footsteps that bring a thirsty traveler to a dry well,
Let the seasons return with the bees that feed on blossom, my love.

If you delight in dancing, I will clear a spot in the cloistered hills
Where sunbirds range and ochre is abundant. When you take to
The arena and ride over the evening with a parasol of your brilliance
People will say who taught her the skills required for such grace
For you'll dance with the passion of your soul. And I like a gazelle
That waits in the undergrowth for the rising sun, will linger to watch.

Burn notice

There is a cabinet in the house crammed with old letters
From years past, and photographs fading at the edges.
I found a photograph with a 'burn' notice mark
Of Maria in a wedding dress, and I in a suit
Basking at a fire by an anthill in a chilly morning breeze.
It was a wedding church rehearsal, I recalled,
The whole village assembled by the anthill side.
I looked at the smudged photograph for a long time.
Then, with mustered courage, gathered all the photographs
And old letters that reminded me of that chilly church rehearsal
And took them to a hollow by the *msolo* tree at the base
Of the anthill once used as an altar by those who came before us
To induct the young into village customs of marriage rites;
It is to that same hollow spot that I now retired with old letters
And faded photographs of my erstwhile wife.
I gathered firewood into the hollow, put a match to it,
And discharged into the bonfire all the pieces of failed dreams
And reminders of scenes where love could have happened;
I stood back and watched raging flames curl out into
Evening air, burning everything indiscriminately.
It was a ritual, I was sure, the ancients also performed
To cleanse their villages of sorcery and evil, and rekindle
In the youth a nascent mistrust of professed life of virtue
And arranged marriage. A surge of childish ecstasy rose in me,
For I needed such a ritual to remove all traces of the fated church
Ceremony, that long ago, and the priestly promises of matrimonial
Bliss, served to the faithful young men and women
Forced to accept the wishes of their elders.
Everything promised was betrayed by the routine
Of existence, and soon Maria and I parted ways at the turn
Where the road forked into a narrow and less used paths.
Although the lonely journey has been heavy at heart, I say
No path should be traveled twice, even with a noble cause.
I rose to go. It had to be, I thought. It had to be done.

But standing back, watching the well-slacked fire
I felt an uneasiness in my limbs, a nag at my conscience,
A thudding awareness that the history of my life
Has just been burned out of existence, that at
My age I could not emerge as a blank slate.
At the same time, however, I couldn't walk into the future
Encumbered by a past savored in those burned mementos.
There was an after-taste welling up in me
That maybe I should have burned more
Than just the old letters and faded photographs –
I should also have burned down the damned church
We got married in, the vestments used in the ceremony,
And cut down the *msolo* tree where the elders sat,
For my marriage was the worst mistake of all.
After all these years, a part of me still grieves
For the young man desirous of the bliss promised
By the equivocating priest, and the peace and harmony
Proclaimed by the venerated elders, knowing I could not
Live the one life without burning the other.

The parting

She was a buxom lady, if ever there was one,
A prideful sight at village gatherings in her prime
A bubbly and beautiful lady, whichever way you looked.
So I fell in love with her, head over heels
And frolicked the hills with flirt abandon
Trailing her undulations everywhere.

But when she turned religious and started mumbling
About hell fire and brimstone I knew she en-figured tragedy.
I knew also that there was no empathy left between us
For we were both too bent to our ways, too
Counterpoised to be dedicated to each other, and so I quit.

Citing cruelty and incompatibility because of insanity,
The judge pronounced our parting and decreed her due.
I knew people would talk and say it's because of
Her wont of intellect and artistic flair, or infidelity
On my part, but I deny it. I had lain naked besides her
And she was familiar with my birthmarks.

The one I love was not there

I went over hills and across rivers,
Went down the valleys, crisscrossed
The countryside, wading through
Reedy swamps, and creeks,
But the one I love was not there.

I rose with dawn, searched until dusk
I pined with loneliness,
Fed only on dew and honey,
The one I love was not there.

I went to the hermit on an anthill
Have you seen her? I asked.
He looked blurry eyed and blank
The one I love was not there.

When the moon was out the hermit reemerged
With herbs of the wandering maid
Fragrant like flowers in the field;
He said the one I love could not be found.

Printed in the United States
By Bookmasters